To Leila
a great poet
a great friend.
with my best wishes.

Playing God

Marty Gervais.
Oct '94

Playing God

Poems by C. H. Gervais

Mosaic Press
Oakville - Buffalo - London

Canadian Cataloguing in Publication Data

Gervais, C.H. (Charles Henry), 1946-
    Playing God

ISBN: 0-88962-580-8

I. Title.

PS8563.E7P53 1994   C811'.54   C94-931768-3
PR9199.3.G47P53 1994

No part of this book may be reproduced or transmitted in any form, by any means, electronic or mechanical, including photocopying and recording information storage and retrieval systems, without permission in writing from the publisher, except by a reviewer who may quote brief passages in a review.

Published by MOSAIC PRESS, P.O. Box 1032, Oakville, Ontario, L6J 5E9, Canada. Offices and warehouse at 1252 Speers Road, Units #1&2, Oakville, Ontario, L6L 5N9, Canada and Mosaic Press, 85 River Rock Drive, Suite 202, Buffalo, N.Y., 14207, USA.

Mosaic Press acknowledges the assistance of the Canada Council, the Ontario Arts Council, the Ontario Ministry of Culture, Tourism and Recreation and the Dept. of Communications, Government of Canada, for their support of our publishing programme.

Copyright © C.H. Gervais, 1994

Cover and book design by
Printed and bound in Canada
ISBN

In Canada:
    MOSAIC PRESS, 1252 Speers Road, Units #1&2, Oakville, Ontario, L6L 5N9, Canada. P.O. Box 1032, Oakville, Ontario, L6J 5E9
In the United States:
    Mosaic Press, 85 River Rock Drive, Suite 202, Buffalo, N.Y., 14207
In the U.K.
    John Calder (Publishers) Ltd., 9-15 Neal Street, London, WC2 H9TU, England

The author wishes to thank the faith of a number of individuals who encouraged me in the writing of this book. These include Karen Mulhallen, Howard Aster, Paul Vasey, Geoff Hancock, John Flood, Greg Gatenby and many others, including the hospital staff at Metropolitan Hospital who found it amusing to find me up in the middle of the night working on these poems when I should have been paying more attention to recovery. Thanks also must go to such magazines and publishing houses as Descant, Mosaic, and Penumbra who directed funds to me through the Writers' Reserve program of the Ontario Arts Council. Some of these poems, in earlier drafts, appeared in Descant. Finally, thanks must also go to Judith Fitzgerald who made me reassess everything I wrote.

This book is dedicated to Donna

Take your good works and be gone . . . I'll take my flute, the stars at night, my few books, the psalms. I'll manage somehow.
- Fr. Matthew Kelty, Trappist monk at Gethsemani

Simplify, simplify . . .
- Thoreau, Walden

TABLE OF CONTENTS

1

Thomas Merton's Picture High Above My Desk   9
To Wash The Soul   10
Cold Happy Stars   12
The Way Heavenly Bodies Exist   22
Lenten Prayers   23
The First Lady   33

2

The Last Pie   38
The Barber Shop   40
Another One In Hell   42
After The Rain   44
In That Voice   49
Where We Might Land Up   50
Dark Sounds of Night   52
The Chicken Farmer   53
Sometimes It Is Better   55
Their Song After Winter   57
Natural Acts   58
The Affairs of Death   62
Neat and Tidy Endings   63
Harlow On A Cold Morning   66
How To Write About Love   67

3

French Sky   70
Notes From A Daughter   71
Thieves in Provence   72
Pair Of Pants In Paris   74
Tango With The Archangel   75
Views Of The Seine   76
Carpet Salesmen   89
Playing God   95

1

Thomas Merton's Picture High Above My Desk

Thomas Merton smiles on all the chaos:
    one young son asleep on the chair beside me
        another doing homework in the other room
    the youngest asleep at long last
in a downstairs room
      The other rooms now lay silent
with pots, Tupperware, Lego scattered about

To Wash The Soul

It seems Herbert Hoover
worried more
over the depths
of trout pools than
neighbors in Alabama
tarpaper shacks
It seems he found
the time to ponder
the importance
of fly fishing
and likened it to a
struggle with the
soul, bathing
in its purity
its simplicity
its need
for patience
and accuracy
It seems he
compared fly-fishing
to prayer but believed
praying wasn't something
you could do all day
It seems we're so
caught up in
one thing or another
and forget the boundaries
Thomas Merton yearned
for the dark hours
in the prayer stall but
rushed among a hundred
monks as the monastery barn
went up in flames,
realizing that beyond
prayer lies something
fundamental,

a fine balancing
point, a boundary between
what is possible and sensible,
between crisis and faith

Cold Happy Stars

1. Arriving just after compline
at the monastery
    telling the guest master
how I'd taken the wrong road,
went missing in the fog.
    No matter:
key to a room
  in the dark
    bells as the community makes
its way to rest
    only the faint scatter of rain
 a soul that revs like an old car engine

2. Night of awful dreaming
    skipping vigils, setting the alarm
        to get up at lauds

Finally waking
    pulling on clothes
snatching up a Psalter
    Late!
  Taking my place at the back
    Remembering the first time here -
    midst of summer, crushing humidity
  Merton's line about rain
after vespers
  cool easy grace of that moment
monks standing in a summer shower
    Now the cold, bone-chilling
this morning where you can feel a storm
coming up
    Returning to retrieve a sweater
  No matter, there's little wrong here
Merton says it's a place free from variations
 . . . *Only what heaven takes into itself
can cause change, nothing else . . .*

I recognize faces from before
    same brothers bowing
in the darkened sanctuary before dawn
 same even, slow, meditative calm
beginning the day,

3. At breakfast, a steaming bowl of oatmeal
juice, tea, lemon cake,
   a coming home
     then sleeping an hour
as rain turns to snow
   waking to a room
floor of scattered books and papers
   What am I trying to figure out?

Walking on nearby hills
  Return to notice the guest master at a desk facing the road
    his floor littered with memos as he balances
 a year's bookings

    On the crucifix above him
Christ shrugs; religion has come down
to this, the business of a Holiday Inn

Downstairs a monk
  at the switchboard reads,
     hood shrouding a grizzled face

  wind whipping through open door,
ajar because a retreatant's insistence
  on smoking in the lobby

"I wonder if there's any way of inventing
something to get the smell of smoke
    out of a room," he says simply

5. Music of Erik Satie,
chocolate pudding at dinner
   Sun fading from slate-gray winter sky

Carrying hot tea back to my room
  blinds opened to outlying hills
darkening like shapes under an eiderdown
At vespers earlier: clear voices of monks
  praising the routine to which they cling
      The surprises within

Reading how Merton
    rising at dawn one day caught sight
of Mars, red red Mars hanging,
     a tiny artificial fruit from a topmost branch of a bare tree

6. The whir of a motorized chair
   at various offices -- this brother
crewcut and broad-smiling face
           having pulled on a white robe over a
       University of Kentucky sweatshirt

Told me before --
    the years have gone pretty fast
since coming here 41 years ago
   Then 15:
"I think they said, 'That's it! No more!'"
     That unmistakable smile

     At compline, don't notice him
in the candle-lit church
  to praise Mary, believe the stark white walls
    lift him, a mother in that moment
as monks file past the abbot for nightly blessing

Later: Fr. Matthew Kelty, the guest-house chaplain
   reads Yeats and Pound and Frost
   and a homily from years before
about a monk who left Gethsemani
 but returned with AIDS
    petitioning the abbot to let him be buried there

   A white cross outside the church
     offers the man's name

7. At the window
   a north wind whips across the landscape
bearing the faint smell of hickory smoke
  and a sky full of (what Merton called)
    those cold happy stars

[*"cold terrible stars"* — depends on the mood!]

8. Difficulty of getting up for vigils
   in the cold sanctuary
ill prepared for dampness
   - the dilemma Merton faced in those first years
when the monks slept on straw
    Kept each other awake at night with snoring
     Merton put it this way: *"I see nothing, I understand nothing!"* (The Sign of Jonas)

9. After mass and breakfast
  drawing up the blinds in my room
     watching the sun rise
 over the barns
   then falling promptly back to sleep
    Later waking in a room full of sunlight
   Taking the path by the monastery wall
down the road ---
   finding another path in the woods
to Monk's Pond shimmering in January light
   sound of bluejays in the cedars

Further down -- swarms of crows
descending upon frayed remains
　　of a corn field

10. Lunch -
　　　Merton on tape
　　talking to novices about pains, scars
about feeling what's not *really* there,
　　a leg that's been amputated
　　　　a ghost sensation.
Hurts, anxieties, obsessions
　　plague and dog us long after events.
They're what's real

11. A day of talk --
　　those who once knew Father Louis
　one brother spoke to him
just before he left for southeast Asia
　　securing a promise Merton would set up
a program for lay brothers

12. Reading into the night
　　Merton at the hermitage
　　　eschewing the old decor of habits,
　stalls, stained glass
　*all so unreal when you've been praying
psalms among the pine trees.* (Vow of Conversation)

　　　There among the heat of summer
picnicking in the grass
　　beer and sandwiches
longhaired Joan Baez talking nonviolence
　singing together

   There sneaking out with friends
for rendezvous in Louisville
  full of guilt
    writing letters to say so
boyishness of it all

   There splitting logs, gathering
  pine cones for a fire
   before dawn warming hands
and saying lauds
followed by mass in an adjacent room

   There writing in the journals
complaining about the monastery's distancing
   itself from essentials
the cold and the woods and the stars . . .

   Yet last night Fr. Kelty argued
  these are still the same monks
hoeing gardens
 wrapping cakes
   feeding cattle

still doing the things they've always done
 in order to push the sun and the moon
  to come up each day, each night, each
day, each night

13. This morning the monastery is cold
At vespers, monks wear woolen sweaters
  over habits
warming hands in deep pockets
before turning pages in the Psalter

hot porridge and tea
  in the darkness of the refectory

    waiting for light --
    watching the sun mount the deckle-edged
pines and barns and wondering why
 it all seems so spectacular
"*I see nothing; I understand nothing.*"

14. Trying to keep warm
       cupping a mug of tea
catching sight of cardinals in the grass
   near the church scrapping over
 scattered bread

   Merton speaks of being *in the clear*,
finding this place
    where he learns to sleep again
The trees I know; the night I know; the rain I know.
   (*Rain and the Rhinoceros*)

   There, this sense of comfort
of knowledge, of having found peace in new routine
    away from the monastery

    There, Merton making his way to the hermitage
 sun going down and saying vespers
   making porridge on a Coleman stove
listening to rain

   There, the ambiguity of *anguish and certitude*"
   (*Vow of Conversation*)
fighting with the abbot
   desperately wanting to travel
      silently mouthing complaints in diaries and letters

> There, watching the rain engulf the flat-roofed building
> in the woods, like *speech pouring down,*
> *selling nothing, judging nobody, drenching the thick mulch*
> *of dead leaves . . . this wonderful, unintelligible,*
> *perfectly innocent speech . . .* (Rhinoceros)

Being in the clear
    buffeted by this obsession for living
       There, sweeping out the hermitage for guests
the real meaning of being the hermit,
preparing for the world at your doorstep

       There, confounded by the days, the intellectual pride
of feeling unjustly treated, exploited
    reverting to fasting
    It clears the head, lessens anguish . . . brings order.
        (*Vow of Conversation*)

Mid afternoon --
    stealing into the refectory for brown bread and peanut
        butter
sitting at a long wooden table to read
    Merton's observation of the sense of futility
in a spiritual life, of assuming one becomes
    a person without problems
       In those first years at the hermitage
1964: seeing how he could easily *fall apart.*

      There: "*I talk to myself, I dance around the hermitage,*
I sing . . .It is the manifestation of weakness, of dizziness . . ."
    (*Vow of Conversation*)
Next day realizing: "*One must pray or go to seed . . .*"

     There, hearing the guns at Fort Knox
or sudden disruption as bombers swoop

low over the trees:
"I could see the trap doors of the bomb bays."

But there's always silence, snow,
    fire in the hearth
the moment at lauds
walking back to the hermitage:
    . . everything there, stars and light,
frost and cold, ice and snow, trees, earth, hills
and cosy in the lighted monastery, the sons of men . . .

    There, more battles with Dom James
wishing to distance himself, refusals to let him
    go to Japan, to go anywhere

      Curiosity --
    now both dead
Merton, first, 1968
    Dom James, 1989

    their crosses side by side
in the winter grave yard by the church

    Br. Patrick Hart, Merton's former secretary
smiles when I ask about it before compline:
"Monastic irony, I guess."

15. Barn swallows rushing from the cold buildings
    at the top of the hill
 at daybreak
    Bells along the great sweep

Running down to Gethsemani
    sun winking above spires
Each one of the men fills a bowl with porridge
    offers thanks

THE WAY HEAVENLY BODIES EXIST

You exist, you think, the way
the heavenly bodies exist . . .
- Maps, Nurudden Farah

I am better organized now
It seems everything --
for that matter -- everyone
is at my disposal
No longer a problem
finding time
The difficulty lies
in finding words

Yet I am
here to gather up
memories, thoughts
finding nothing to say
finding even beauty repellent
Believe me, it's true,
I am not certain why
Scattered about this hotel room:
books and newspapers
I can hardly finish a paragraph
prefer to stare
at the television
shut off

LENTEN PRAYERS

1. Ash Wednesday:
an old chaplain thumbs
a broad cross
on my
forehead
my brain
swilling
in a haze
of morphine
a day
after
abdominal
surgery
Somehow
the cross
stills me
its ashes
alive
murmuring
gossip
prayers

2. It is always
the first thing
I see:
the ceiling
of the hospital
room,
a morning,
a summer
sky, a
day of
possibilities,
boyhood,
innocence,
its soft
embrace
its warmth,
the wool
blanket
draped over
my feet

3. There's little else
to think about
My words are clear:
Lift the pain just long enough
for me to feel
comfort
long enough
to finish this article
in the paper
long enough
to brush my teeth
long enough
to move across the room
to catch the last light
of winter
outside
these four walls

4. Wake with an anxiety
an annoyance
that accompanies
moments alone
Sounds of hospital routine,
life sustaining machines
that drag you
through days,
staring blankly at solid colors
that over time hover
and twist into shapes no longer
real, human
I descend to them,
embrace them,
wonder if there's a way out,
something to love,
In those moments
I mouth the words,
let me return
this is not defeatism
but a yearning
for the familiar,
the known

5. I clutch the narrow copper cross
from the Roman catacombs
through the night
Stabbing pain
with even the slightest movement
from one side of the bed
to the other
Morphine intravenous drips
into me like punchlines
to old movies
But it is this tiny icon
that carries me
through the darkness
lets me wait
for the light at the
window
for that
first visitor

6. The pain
an old friend
keeps you near
keeps you at a necessary distance
in the knowledge
it cannot be endured
alone,
keeps you promising
never to embrace
those old vices
if only it would lift now
But this friend's fickleness
keeps the yearning pure
sends you in search of
freedom,
a moment of grace,
blessed time out

7. An afternoon
of dreaming:
the *Baltimore Catechism*
Lenten rules say
nothing of the pain
its geography
its territory
its lurid veined map
an adventure
where we know
the beginning
It isn't only
the ending
we fear
We take *this* path
or *another*
in spite of ourselves
clearly marked as
we move from
the centre outward
The mystery
lies in the question of arrival
inevitability
Today, this first
Sunday of Lent
it finds me alive
incandescent
aglow
astride this highway
clicking off
the miles
I mouth a silent prayer:
Make me tougher
Make me human

8. Awake at night,
the pain nearly
there but for
the drug that has
relaxed its grip
tricked it,
made it sleep
Beyond the far
windows
I glimpse
a dark city, asleep
uncaring, unaware
There's nothing
I want to read
to see, to eat
to do, to hear
except for the
winter storm
that murmurs
its comfort
against the nightly
routine

9. In the midst
of such confusion
I feel their presence
alive
brushing past the bed
moving about
with blankets
faces so
clear and familiar
I want to ask them
about sorrow
about truth
love, anger
joy, real joy
about
the other side
In the morning
the nurses seem
confused by my desire
to learn
who might
have covered me
in the night
who might
have brought me
water in a China cup
from downstairs

10. A friend
shuts the door
helps me back to bed
tells me to shut
my eyes
to let go
to fall away,
hypnotizes me,
urges me
to heal myself
to place at my disposal
those tools
to ease the pain
to feel alive
My mind tumbles
into noises, far
away neighborhoods
It struggles with
a few Latin words
from my boyhood
as an altar boy
My body
seems to float
there above
a white clapboard
church, those
moments in preparation
before stepping out
to celebrate mass,
faint odors of
incense, floor wax
and Old Spice
I hover long enough
to see the pain
evaporate
hands clasped
in prayer

The First Lady

She's been at Gethsemani
for ten weeks, already
making waves, sporting a
sharp-tongue and severe grimace
as she cleans up in
the kitchen --
the first woman
hired by the monastery in
its 145-year history
She doesn't like
what she sees
You can tell when
there's not a woman
around -- things just
aren't clean like
they should be
stated in that southern
drawl at a long
wooden table
in the bowels
of the monastery
just down a sloping
corridor from
the refectory
where she serves
the retreatants
She talks and smokes like
there's no tomorrow,
doesn't hesitate to
tempt monks
with trying cigarettes --
Go for it she taunts
A Latin American priest
actually accepts one,
rolls and flips it like
he used to when he

was a boy but reluctantly
returns it to the package
Kathleen's her name,
a Kentuckian who
resides five miles down
the road and someone
they trust -- indeed
they're fond of her, not
afraid of asking
what's the best way to
cut up a chicken,
what she'd cook if suddenly
a bus turned up with
a dozen or more guests
What surprises her
is how the monks
discussed her among
themselves before
hiring her and
agreed she should
work for them
yet she knew nothing
about it -- *I hadn't
even applied for a
job. I'm a housewife
and got six kids
so I don't need
this* -- But they
petitioned her husband
a mechanic who'd worked
for the monastery for fifteen years
to ask if she'd take the job
*It was a hoot, let
me tell you and I came in
and told them there was some things
I was going to do*

*and some I wasn't
and yesterday gave them all hell*
They'd prepared
too much porridge
and she had to mop it up
when one of the novices
accidentally dropped
the container on the
floor -- *Have you
ever tried to mop up oatmeal
off a tiled floor? Try it! It'll
drive you nuts!*
But beneath the
scabrous veneer
Kathleen is more a silent fighter
-- maybe even shrewd
or subtle -- and everyone here
knows the story -- how
fifteen years ago
her eighteen-year-old son,
had left Bardstown
one Halloween night
with his buddies
to raise hell and toss eggs at
houses in the country
and as their car
sped away from
one house they had targeted
on the outskirts, someone
from the darkness
fired a .22 calibre
rifle and the bullet ricocheted
and exploded in the boy's brain
Kathleen spent the next
five days at the hospital
praying her heart out

and the night her son
died, it was another
son's birthday
When the inquest was over
she didn't battle the police
or the courts -- they resigned themselves
to yet another unsolved murder
But she knows, knows his identity,
where he works, what kind of
man he is, where he shops,
where he vacations, what church
he goes to Sundays and how
many rifles and pistols there
are in his gun case in that house
on the edge of town -- she's
made it her business

2

The Last Pie

I go down to Sorrento's on Erie Street
a café that bakes pizza in large silver ovens
just on the other side of the wall
from a smoky room crammed
with snooker tables and where
the television roars with
Sunday afternoon soccer games
I study a swarthy man slice
through the steaming pizza with
a pair of garden shears
and place each slice into a cardboard box--
not the sort of pizza, neat and triangular
but irregular, uneven
Then I drive home to meet my father
and sister who have come over dinner
Kids everywhere -- hockey nets
baseball bats, scattered toys across rooms,
the sort of chaos that makes you
want to walk right back out to the car,
drive straight through to Alabama
or some place with a quiet motel
But you step into it, smiling
because you know your fate,
nodding to everyone, breaking
open the box, letting hands at the pizza
It's hard to focus on anything
in particular, to listen to anyone
for more than a few seconds
My sister is holding up something, and saying
she has brought ginger ale
I nod absent mindedly with thanks
but she's holding up something
not a bottle, but a pie and tells me
again, but it's not ginger ale that
she's saying, it's a pie, a pie that
our mother made six or eight months

ago -- it's been in the freezer all that time
and it makes you pause because our mom
died about a month and a half ago
She had been in the hospital
and a day before she died, she'd promised
she was going to make me a pie
and you'd have to know my mom,
just how positive she was,
how she believed in things that couldn't possibly
happen -- and often didn't -- but she persisted
in this faith, and there she was dying, assuring
me she was going to get out of the hospital
and bake me a pie
I know it doesn't make any sense,
but there I am at the end of August,
just a few weeks from what would be her birthday
and I'm cutting into a piece of that apple pie
I know it doesn't make any sense
but it makes you wonder if she was right all along

The Barber Shop

Saturday mornings
at the barber shop
on Wyandotte
heads bowed, absorbed
in comic books, we sit,
wait our turn
on the broad window ledge
or in upright chrome
and leather covered chairs
occasionally tear out coupons,
believing we'll get rich,
fatten our biceps
become recording stars.
Buzz cuts for summer
trims for winter
and, always that moment
of elation over graduating
from the painted board
across the arm rests
of the barber's chair
to the cracked soft leather seat
the seat of adult talk,
ponderous, male:
Korea, trials at Nuremberg,
Ike's golf game, trade
of Rocky Colavito to
the Tigers, the Sputnik
Bored, me lose yourself
in the multicolored bottles
atop shelves near the mirror
behind the barber,
absorbed in the pungent odors
of hair tonics wafting up like
the smell of a new scribbler
in September.
It was the fifties and we dreamed

of sideburns, and I took
my mom's eyebrow pencil
and drew wide-slanting strips
down my cheeks
confident no one would
notice they were fake
For a time, I actually believed
I had the same lips as Elvis,
and stood endlessly at the mirror
studying that trademark sneer.
Those Saturday mornings
we lived imaginary lives
as the bow-tied barber's scissors
fanned over our head
and sure, we did stupid things
and I did stupid things, and sure
we even dreamed stupid things.

ANOTHER ONE IN HELL

Never quite as bold as them, never quite
as daring, I preferred to stay closer to home
to sit on the steps of the verandah
on a summer's day while my brothers ventured
fearlessly into nearby construction sites
fitting their thin bodies into cramped
caverns among cables and pipes
of a new school, crawling on hands and knees
and carrying flashlights down
dark muddy tunnels in search of rats, treasures
Really at nine, I had no choice but to lie,
to wait on the wide wooden steps
with a nearby radio, hoping Bertoia
of the Tigers would stay ahead of Williams
in the batting race so early in the season,
then telling my mom I didn't know where Billy
was, or anyone else, that maybe they'd wandered
down to *Cooties* the confectionery on Wyandotte,
then worried myself sick over lying, troubled if
I didn't get to confession before Saturday
I might die and go straight to the Devil
Somehow it seemed more real
for we actually knew someone who'd gone to Hell
someone from Windsor, Ont.
I mean we figured Hitler had; we figured Elvis
was on his way -- at least from what the priest
was saying after seeing him on Ed Sullivan
It silenced us all one July afternoon
when we learned my oldest brother's best buddy,
unloading crates at a warehouse, had been killed
by a truck that slipped out of gear and crushed him
It had been a Monday morning, first thing,
and we knew the day before he'd raided
a farmer's orchard, had filled the trunk of his Merc'
with apples, and had no chance
of ever getting to confession

In fact, he'd been over at our house that night
long after Ed Sullivan, boasting how he'd filched
these apples right under the nose
of the doting old farmer
That Monday afternoon I read about him
in the *Star*, pored over the article, couldn't keep
my eyes off the picture of the truck,
the graduation photo
It was then Billy told me he must've gone
straight to Hell, that he just might've been
the first one from the neighborhood

AFTER THE RAIN
For all the neighbors

1

A rainy morning in the spring
when we saw the place
Just one walk-through
made us decide to buy it --
a one-room school
at a crossroads of a hamlet
long ago having
sunk into obscurity
A month later
we moved in, discovering
how we hadn't noticed
there was no running water
no well, indeed, no
hope of one
I didn't find out
the whole story
until seeing old Mister Donais
down the gravel road --
At one time he supplied
water to this school
There, sitting in his kitchen
the two of us on rocking chairs
side by side, drinking coffee
he asks what I've asked myself
a thousand times already,
"So what're you going
to do about water?"
"I guess that's why I'm here."
"I can't give you any," he says flatly.
"I'm supplyin' my boys
and there's only enough for us!
So what'll you do?"
"Guess it means digging a well."
"A well? Where're you goin' to put it?"

"I don't know -- I'll get in a well-digger
and let him decide."
"Nothing to decide -- they've
witched it . . . There's nothing!
They've dug everywhere
There's nothing." That's that
We rock back and forth
in the gloom of the kitchen --
listen to the rain falling on
the tin roof of the nearby shed,
say nothing till Mister Donais speaks:
"You got a big roof over there!"
At that we both stop rocking,
hunch forward in our chairs,
stare out the window
down the road at the schoolhouse
Yup, I say to myself, it's a big roof
but what in hell does that mean?
I nod and wait for an explanation,
Hell, pray for one
Instead, the old farmer mutters again:
"Yessir that's one big roof you got!"
I don't have the foggiest idea
what he means till he fetches
his pipe, turns to me, and asks,
"Have you ever thought about the rain?"
I'm relieved he'd changed the subject
But what the hell, we've gone
from roofs to rain. What does he mean?
Is this some kind of philosophical equation
he's wanting me to crack?
I just want water in my house
The old farmer knows he's dealing
with a bone head
"A cistern!" he informs me,
then lights his pipe and puffs deeply

Suddenly, it all makes sense:
collecting rain water from the roof
Yes, and with that I take off home
finally with all the answers

2

Building the cistern?
Something else again
It was apparent I'd become *entertainment*
for the few scattered families
among the concession roads
It's not uncommon for farmers
to pull up by the side of road
to check out the action, the comedy,
and naturally they were curious
how I'd get it done
There I was, hiring someone to build the tank
and sink it into the ground
But before digging, he asks where I'd like it
Standing by the side of the house
facing it, watching my young daughter
playing at the window, I turn around
and point to the poplar tree near the fence
With that, the well digger swings around,
kind of pushes back the cap on his head,
raises an eyebrow, and asks, "Over there?"
There, being about seventy to eighty
feet from the building
"Yeah, I think so."
He shrugs, and hauls in equipment
to dig the hole and sink the form
into the ground, then advises me --
as did all neighboring farmers
who'd gathered around the hole --
it'd be best to put in

galvanized piping to link
the cistern to the house
"With galvanized, you'll never
have trouble -- it'll be there
forever. You'll never
have to dig again!"
I drive to town, ask for
eighty feet of galvanized --
it's going to cost me hundreds of dollars
I return to measure, buy the piping
but wait till dusk to link the well to the house
then quickly cover the trench
Five years later, I sell the house
move to the city
Another rainy spring morning
when I get a call from the new owners:
"We've checked everything,
and we can't figure out why we're
not getting any water
The pump seems to be working fine,
the well is full and we know it's not the
line, because everybody around here
says you put in galvanized,
so it can't be that
What do you suppose it is?"
I blush, feeling as if I'd just been
caught burying a dead baby in the garden
I want to confess how I'd ignored
the warnings -- some even claimed
they'd seen me covering up
the line, swore up and down
the line was galvanized, boasted
nothing short of nuclear war

could destroy it
But after a long pause I concede
it's not the pump or anything else
It's probably the line --
I hadn't used galvanized after all
Instead I buried cheap rubber hosing,
Not only that, but had to piece it together
because I'd measured with a wooden ruler
and prayed for five successive winters
that somehow, somehow
the line would hold, and
nothing would go wrong

In That Voice
For Marie-Anne Mineau

Your weakened voice
carries inflections of some
other time, perhaps
when you were
on the farm
as a young girl
perhaps when you
were happiest
hastening along
gravel roads
after school
near Pointe-au-Roaches
there, under ice-grey sky
trailing your sister,
calling after her
to wait up, wind
slapping your face
muffling your words
This afternoon
at the hospital I wonder
about that time, about
you, what you had to
say then, how you might
have sounded
In your eyes there is
someone desperate to voice
their love, to hang
on to this time,
this hour, this day

Where We Might Land Up

I can remember that afternoon
that summer, standing in the backyard
with our daughter, everyone inside
rushing about getting ready
for your sister's wedding
Your father bewildered, standing
and staring out the back window
Your mother barking at you and your sister
as the last moments ticked down
before going to church
Our daughter concerned only
with getting on and off the swing
Days like that I could bundle her
into the car, leave for good
no explanation, just shut the doors
and drive away
Your father might've felt the same
those years wondering why he'd left Texas
to come north to this country
to work on a railroad and raise a family
Might've said something to the other yardmen
those gray winter afternoons

in the caboose at the New York Central yards
in Detroit when he'd cook up a kettle
of chili and bake corn bread
But probably not, for he kept so much
to himself, cared tremendously
for his own, displayed a fierce loyalty
As for your mother, and her relationship
with him, there was a kind of resignation,
a settling back, believing in no way out
Then again, why should there be?
There was always the choice
ever out of one's grasp --
yet the feeling there could be
time to work out details, changes
That afternoon I chose to pursue
our daughter, chose to ponder
only questions, ignore decisions
leaving it to the gods where
we might all land up one day

The Dark Sounds of Night

Dark sounds of night
As a coming storm
rolls over a landscape of factories
subdivisions to the east
Up to shut the windows
Curtains billow out
with cool air --
remnants of a humid
spring night in early June

In moments like these
we talk of our parents,
their ghosts moving
in the thin air of night:
a shoe dropping on the floor above
a whisper of wind at the sills

You ask me to close the door
of the bedroom
You recall your father
fitting a fattened Rothmans cigarette package
between the door and the jam
to stop the jostling sounds

Now we let go,
prefer the delicate knocking,
a familiar voice

THE CHICKEN FARMER

After the funeral --
the only time
we get together --
gravitating to this
one moment
in grief:
the K of C Hall
banquet tables
buffet style cold cuts, salads,
shaking hands
retelling the same stories
There among this
scattered disjointed family funeral,
the smiling chicken farmer
my mother's half brother,
-- never adopted -- but
taken in by my grandmother
when his own mother
hanged herself
in the closet of
an upstairs' bedroom
in the ramshackle farmhouse
near Stony Point,
an event rarely mentioned
still scandalous
though it happened
seventy years ago
There among them
offering condolences,
the brilliant smile, a new story
Today, how once
he was the only one to
turn out for a cousin's
funeral, except for
the priest and the
funeral director --

a winter in the fifties
how they had to stop
someone on the main street
shovelling snow to ask
if they'd pallbear,
how they'd gone down
to the post office, recruited
others, strangers
"No one really liked
him . . . I didn't even like
him," said my uncle,
"but I thought should
go." Maybe, it's that
about him, his presence
always assured,
stepping in, stiff Sunday suit,
ever the chicken farmer,
ever the one just on
the edge of that moment
out of harm's way,
survivor of a brilliant
summer day, abandoned
by a mother, mad
-- not at him
but with a world of obligations,
maybe the heat of
the day, or just with
the way things are

Sometimes It Is Better

It is better to stay here
better to dream about running,
of poring over maps
planning escapes,
setting schedules, goals,
and rationalizing
But when it's time to leave,
it's probably better to stay
Like this morning
Maybe I've taught my children
the wrong things --
A daughter slams down the phone
in frustration over a friend's betrayal
An oldest son swears over changing pedals
on his bike in the driveway
sweating in the hot sun
calling his mom for help,
not me; no use -- I sit in a room
at the back of the house, ignore it all,
reading, dreaming, doing nothing
Remember boyhood summers
on the back porch, daydreaming,
and my mother urging me
to the lake, to get out in the sun
Today I hear my son's words
My own as an adult:
angry, frustrated, crude.

Why didn't they learn
their mother's gentleness, patience?
Other times I recognize another
side of me, something at the centre --
someone calm, tasteful, articulate,
like words written with a fountain pen
clean, composed, familiar
Even the smell
of wet ink stills me
Why can't they see that?

THEIR SONG AFTER THE WINTER

One of those nights
Up a dozen
times, mesmerized by
the motionless darkness
out the front window
Empty-headed
Exhausted
Unable to sleep
Comforted suddenly
by the sound
of morning doves
whose songs at this early hour
remind me they're back
after the winter
Then again
Maybe I've simply ignored them
all this time

Natural Acts

1.

Why do I feel so compelled
to lie when I'm wakened
by the telephone
in the middle of the night
and asked if I've just gotten
out of bed?
Why do I say I've been awake
all along even though
the caller can detect
from my voice
I've just been pulled
from a deep sleep?
Why lie?

2.

It was *always*
easy to confess
to the priest that you lied
Actually, it was customary
to use lies to pad out
a confession, to cushion bigger sins
"I disobeyed my mother four times,
talked back to her two times . . .
fooled around with my girlfriend . . .
LIED sixteen times . . ."

3.

Barely five years old
I lied about my mother's
diamond ring
All through a long
humid summer morning
pestered with questions

about whether I'd gone
into my parents' dresser
filched my mother's
wedding ring
I finally admitted
to the act
though knew I hadn't
taken anything
Just got tired of
interrogation
It occurred to me
if I simply confessed
they'd quit nagging
Instead a flurry
of new questions
even more urgent:
Where did I put it?
What did I do with it?
Where was it?
So I blurted out the truth
They didn't believe me
Still more questions:
Why had I told them
I took it if I had not?
Was I lying?
So, I confessed again
confessed to snatching
the ring from
my mother's dresser,
to carrying it down
to the railway tracks,
to letting a train run over it,
to watching it smash
to smithereens
Now it was gone forever . . .
Surely, that was the end of it?
No: What train?

When did I do this?
Yesterday? This morning?
When? Was
there really a train?
Again, I tried the truth.
If it was true I hadn't
stolen it, why would I
bring up the railway
tracks and the train?
They didn't believe me
They believed the lies
Somehow they *knew*
I'd taken it somewhere
hidden it, lost it, fed it
to the dog, flushed it
down the toilet
After a while, I no longer
knew the truth
So, I'd start
all over again,
acknowledged stealing
the ring . . .
After a while, I simply
didn't know
That evening my mother
accidentally stumbled upon
the ring, found it wrapped in
one of her scented handkerchiefs
in a corner cabinet
in the kitchen . . . It looked
like my kind of work

4.

"Be true to yourself."
Someone told me over
and over again
As a teenager, shuffling
back and forth
on the cement floor
of the basement
of St. Joseph's Church
in Bracebridge, Ont.,
struggling to get
through a speech
fearing I'd forget
everything I was
supposed to say
A self-confidence course
Public speaking
Getting through it
The irony -- believing
more about yourself
than you really believed
knowing it was
all a lie

The Affairs of Death

About an hour after
my mother died
I'm on my hands and knees
in the hospital room
scanning the tiled floor
for one of her tiny pearl earrings
A small boy again
in her bedroom
on Prado Place, that
humid summer of 1950,
kneeling there on the floor
beside her bed
yellow blinds pulled down
my mother yearning to sleep
I can't wake her
I can't wake her
but will she stop sleeping?
There I am this morning
just past dawn, sun barely
wiping its eyes from sleep
my mother's face
far from dreaming
far from all of us now
seeing all
we can't see,
all we fear
I envy that small boy
I treasure his control
This morning
I can't wake her
I can't wake her

June 12, 1992

Neat and Tidy Endings

It is better not to say anything
to simply go about
things in an arbitrary manner
paying little heed to
others' concerns,
when things get
down to the level
of discussions, negotiations,
threats, warnings

A woman in Santa Ana, Calif.
douses her wheelchair-bound
cancer-stricken husband
with rubbing alcohol
and sets him on
fire on Good Friday
after he eats
a chocolate Easter bunny
a friend gives her
The papers report
she's still
so angry
Afterwards
she goes out shopping
for the afternoon

A Georgia man
gets so pissed off at his
wife for changing
the TV channels
he warns her
not to touch
the remote
again

Well, she does
-- not in any sort
of defiant way --
but she does
So he goes off
to the backroom
returns with a hunting
rifle and drills her
in the head

"That'll teach her," he tells the papers

A woman down the
street, so ashamed
the night her teenage daughter
gives birth to a baby
out of wedlock
she takes the newborn
for a ride in a car
and strangles it
waiting for a red light
to change
She returns home
and orders her husband
to bury it in the backyard

"What will our friends think
if they find out our daughter
isn't married and has a baby?"

One hot sticky summer night
a young father
gets to drinking beer
and shakes his crying infant
until it stops suddenly

Next morning
he bundles his bruised
and dead son
into a garbage bag
drives to the Detroit River
and tosses it away

Two teenage sons
angry at their father
because he needs the car
one Friday night
drive him to
a cliff near Big Sur
and tie him
to the steering
wheel before directing
the car over the
dark cliff, yelling
at him, "Hey, it's
your car, Dad! You
drive it!"

Harlow On A Cold Morning

Each morning the same routine

Barely 8 o'clock when
a stout woman from X-Ray
helps me into a wheel chair
to take me downstairs

Conspicuous on the elevator
in hospital gown and black socks

A cool January day
perched in the hallway waiting
my turn, scanning the dark pragmatic rooms
with heavy cables and steel gizmos

It's a large black and white photograph
of Jean Harlow I settle upon --
that stark white innocent gaze
bearing stories in the papers

Bride at 16, bit player at 17,
star at 18, mobster's mistress at 20,
bride again at 21, dead at 26
This sweet woman-child
who bleached her pubic hair
iced her nipples
Why the picture's there on the wall
I can't tell, but there's no denying
those probing eyes, strangely virtuous
how they sweeten an otherwise stark chill

How To Write About Love
(A Found Poem)

1. Best to have people in your stories,
never use real names.
Best to have ideas at work,
not personalities.

2. Stay away from erotica.
Don't use coarse language.
Use metaphors.
Don't complicate things.
Stay away from betrayals,
lies, lost loves.

3. Avoid prefaces,
dedications, specifics.
Just keep circling.

4. Use a lot of foreign words.

5. If you insist upon characters,
let them have all the answers:
Make them clever, witty, worldly.
Let them be in control.
At least one of them
ought to be a woman.

6. It's best never to mention "love,"
never to state it openly;
best to avoid definitions;
being arbitrary
describing scenes that run on at length
with explanations.

7. Keep animals out of your work.
Things get rather silly
with animals.
The same might apply to God,

Art, anything esoteric
(unless you're cynical
then, you'll be seen as
a shrewd observer of modern facts).
Never use a quote about love
from the Bible
--it'll seem contrived.

8. If it's love of country
you're planning to include
avoid using names of political parties.
Abhor the droll mention of taxes
agriculture, the post office, NATO,
the environment, Free Trade, abortion,
Green Peace, federal elections, divorce,
the freedom of information act.

9. If it's "love of power,"
pretend you don't care.
Use a pseudonym.

10. Finally, if it's autobiographical,
forget everything
you've learned,
especially your manners.
Shout out your love clearly
specifically, profanely
from all rooftops
twenty four hours a day.

3

French Sky

The first of it
   I pull back the curtain
bursting in the room
  this smoke-gray day

changing slowly
   perceptibly as I bask in its surprising light
as though I'd mistaken its mood
    for something awry

Tearing French bread
  in this quietude
     just before departing the city

Later, curled in the seat
   of the train to Frankfurt
     catching its face again
a friend anxiously waving goodbye

Saint-Avold, France

Notes From A Daughter

I always search for the notes
in the middle of the night
Get up at two,
at three, at four
Often, a message
near the kitchen sink:
She's come in
momentarily, went out again,
plans to stay with
a friend overnight
take a train to Chatham
With each note
a promise of love

THIEVES IN PROVENCE
For Elise

It's difficult to feel good
about this place; tucked away
in a leather satchel
is a small watercolor
of Provence, its brilliant sun
splashing over the
mountains and the purity of fields
Yet it's here after a day of haggling
with shopkeepers, fighting off
scavengers desperate for handouts,
dodging tap dancing gypsies
or sword swallowers
on streets outside cafés
I return to my rented car
to find the locks jammed
from thieves trying to break in
And after two and one half hours
of battling it out unsuccessfully
with the rental agency
it's apparent with my French
stuck at the level of a five year old
I'm going to get nowhere convincing
them at giving me a new car
So, I flee Aix-en-Provence for Nice,
having had to break into the rental
like a thief because the burglars
have ruined the locks
The Promenade des Anglais
the fountains, the narrow streets
welcome me -- I spend the rest
of the night telephoning home
but find friends splitting up,
kids sick, bills unpaid, my wife bitter
With phone in one hand, and
lying on the bed, I stare out
the window at the rooftops

of this Mediterranean city,
its stars winking their sombre
secrets in the dark night
and realize then what good fortune
has befallen me

Pair of Pants in Paris

She's gone in search
of similar trousers bought
so many years ago
for our sons, gone
to recapture something
of their boyish intimacy
with one another
or the image
of big brother/little brother
or something indefinable
like scanning albums
for a picture to prove
a point, to say you were there
to believe things had to be
a particular way
There was nothing special
about those pants: same color
same pattern, different sizes
They made a statement
about our boys
as does a clever remark
dropped in conversation
and surprises the one
who's made it
They wore those trousers
in the basement of our house,
playing with hockey sticks --
the older son
a magnified shadow moving
a half a step faster
Maybe it's this
my wife recognizes -- this drama,
this affectionate interplay
that speaks inseparability, proving
these two belong to each other

TANGO WITH THE ARCHANGEL
(After a painting by Kees Van Dogen)

She's naked but for red and green shoes
rouge, nylons, lipstick, rings on her right hand
She dances and the stars fall way --
clouds, time, everything
The man she dances with
wears a dark suit, bites her neck
Only after he's moved her effortlessly
into the light, you notice the subtle arc
of his wings, almost dwarfing
the ambient charm. She's lost
She's given her soul over to grace,
to its willingness, its magic
She's the poet dancing on the edge of
innocence, caring not for good, evil,
but the face pressing hers
She embraces darkness believing
in the moment, trusting in the elegant hands
that move her across the cosmos

Views of the Seine

1

SUNDAY AT ARGENTEUIL
(After a painting by Claude Monet)

The sky so big
cluttered with clouds
on this cold day
in spring
Monet has captured
the first sail boats
gliding in
blue stillness
a slight breeze
Friends showing off
in a row boat,
waiting to push
off, one adjusting
an umbrella,
another standing up
holding court,
talking endlessly
about nothing

2

CLAUDE MONET IN HIS STUDIO BOAT AT ARGENTEUIL
(After a painting by Claude Monet)

Not the perfect day --
the tiny boat rocks back
and forth, again a cold morning
The factory stacks puff
out their vileness
but the grass by the river
lies wet and lush after a rain
Monet, seated at the bough,
a canvas anchored in front
of him, paints this
lovely woman who
seems shrouded
perhaps feeling
the spring chill,
shivering, silent,
perhaps wondering
at his selfishness
waiting out the
moment when
they might go to the
café for pernod

3

ON THE SEINE AT BENNECOURT
(*After a painting by Claude Monet*)

Camille has removed
a straw hat, keeping
out of the sun under the shade
of a chestnut tree by the bank
of the river, close
enough to keep an eye
on the row boat moored below
in the shallows
In the distance lies the inn
where her lover has found
lodging for them
but she knows in time
they can't remain there
because there's no money
what with his inability
to sell the paintings
Still, for now there's
the moment, the time together
and the time alone when
she feels most unafraid,
vulnerable

4

BATHERS AT LA GRENOUILLERE
(After a painting by Claude Monet)

Near the end of September,
the water's cold,
and three bathers stand about
on the gangplank making fun
of the others splashing below
Off to one side an assortment
of row boats jostle back and
forth, neglected and solitary
like orphans or dancers
in the nearby halls
There's no money to paint
anything else, and none
of the journalists, scoundrels
or rogues who make their
way west from Paris each week
wish to spend on anything
but women, drinks
Perhaps in Rueil there'll
be someone
Perhaps enough to buy more paints

5

THE SEINE AT BERCY
(*After a painting by Albert Dubois-Pillet*)

Down the cobblestone
to the river this
clear summer
morning
to see the haze
lifting over the bridges
and the men
resting and waiting
to load up the boats
A country weary
of war, ugly patriotism
slumping commerce
and a night we
try to forget
retreating from
other lives,
losing one's self
in a circle of
friends bored
with fighting
And during the
day the painters
seek out their subjects
in what swirls
before them,
Today it has
nothing to do
with politics,
nationalism,
war, anything

serious, just
those boring
clouds billowing
high like the great
cathedrals along
this river, the
colors muted
and subtle
like the china
in the cafés

6

THE BOAT AT GIVERNY
(*After a painting by Claude Monet*)

Evening's falling
and the three young
women fish close
to shore, their
unhappy chatter
carrying easily
in the failing light
One stands in
the boat, a hand
holding the
sagging line,
showing little
interest in
catching anything
The other women
also bored with
the exercise
maybe distraught
over the monotony
of their days in
the big house
What catches
their interest is
the gossip at the
painter's house along
this river, and
curiosity over the
haphazard and
mysterious ways of
his stepson who takes

his small boat
out each evening
at the same
time and
won't return
till the early
hours of
the morning

7

A Summer's Day
(*After a painting by Berthe Morisot*)

You can tell
from the eyes
she's preoccupied
with her lover's
decision
There's nothing to
worry about
she's told
but it matters nothing
what her friend
says,
It matters nothing
that she leans
toward her,
offering all
the right arguments
impressing the
need for self
worth, pride
She feels only the boat
drifting under
the olive sky
this late afternoon
It moves slowly
silently among
the swans
drifting helplessly
away

8

THE SEINE AT PONT D'IENA
(*After a painting by Paul Gaugin*)

That cold evening
in February
Gauguin finished at the bank
anxious to get down
to the river, gathered up
the paint boxes
and made his way down
to the houseboats
covered in snow
His hands freezing
as he hurriedly sketched
the fading light,
the darkening sky
impressed with the
smoke filling the
chill dusk, but worried
over the darkness
somehow believing
it was all wrong
something terrible
like the coldness
he felt toward
those he should
have loved

9

THE ARTIST SKETCHING WITH HIS WIFE
(After a painting by John Singer Sargent)

She leans against his back
looking away from the
picture that he's working on
perhaps bored with the day
disinterested in how his narrow fingers
work the brush over the canvas
Perhaps she doesn't believe him
wonders what the afternoon
might bring when they make
their way back, wonders if
he might lie about his
feelings again, lie about
the things that really
make sense to him
about her, about
the direction their life
might take, wonders
if he's capable of understanding
anything beyond the
pictures he makes of
a world so peaceful

10

SEINE QUAI NEAR PARIS
(After a painting by Armand Guillaumin)

There are days when he misses
the railway yards, at least
the sounds, the heavy
industrial taste in the air
There are times when
he wanders down by the river
near Ivry to watch the coal barges
in the icy Seine,
to talk with the men who stand
by the shore smoking
They seem pleased with their lives
free of politics, free of attachments
resigned to the cold, to the money
hard work along the river
where the sky moves like the
bright skirt of a woman
turning away in the street

11

PONT NEUF
(After a painting by Pierre Auguste Renoir)

Amused at
his brother's enthusiasm
how he went about
stopping people along the bridge
asking them what time it was
where he might find
a certain street, where
he might find the bathing
establishment he knew
lay just below the bridge
at the other end
Renoir sat in the café at the corner
of the quai du Louvre,
furiously sketching those
his brother stopped,
much like the circus hawkers
who worked the crowds
At the end of a long afternoon
Edmond finally
would join him at the café
and fill him in
on all the conversations
the part of the picture
that lay only partly
beyond his grasp

CARPET SALESMEN
For Douglas

1.

First there was Omar
An hour after my arrival
he leads me
to a tiny shop
in a glut of streets
near the Blue Mosque
A young son arrives
with apple tea
as the father launches
into his sales pitch, plying
carpets, spreading each
of them out on the floor,
fetching a butane lighter
to burn the fringe,
and let me smell it
to prove its authenticity
Shows me letters from Canada
from satisfied customers
even a faded Polaroid shot
of a couple from Saskatoon
who bought three last summer
Every now and then
he interjects prices
undaunted as I wave
each of them off quickly
protesting I want
nothing at all
Thanks for the tea, but
I've got to get going
He yanks a wad of American bills
ceremoniously from his pocket,
waves it above his head,
and throws it on the carpeted floor

then stamps on it furiously
Declares this will bring
him good luck, and tells me
the price is now cut in half,
and I shouldn't miss the chance
After all, this carpet will outlast
time, my grandmother, my children
my children's children,
indeed civilization itself
Long after everything has
disappeared, the carpet
bought here in Istanbul
will still be around
I toy with him, asking,
 "Well, how much then
will it cost me?"

2.

My first thought
is she's a hooker --
what with the rouge and lipstick,
leather skirt and brazenness
as she saunters over to my
table in cozy café, asking
if I'm looking for something special
Naturally I'm thinking tits
and ass, at least I'm thinking
that's what she's thinking, but
no, she means leather and carpets
Like everyone else, she's got
her factory, but that's a lie
I tell her I want to finish lunch
Of course, of course, but
moments later she's directing
me down the street to a cramped

basement where they've got
leather jackets half the price
at discount stores in Canada
Again, out comes the butane lighter
singeing the corners of the jackets
Please, please don't burn
the goddamn jackets --
I'll buy one
Of course, this isn't easy
She wants American currency
I protest, asking why
I should pay in American
dollars when I'm Canadian
That's just the way things
are done, everyone pays
in American dollars
So, I ask if Germans and French
pay in American dollars
I'm surprised she falls so easily
into the trap, saying of course,
Europeans don't because
they're not Americans
Well, neither am I,
and tell her if you want me
to buy this jacket,
it'll be in Canadian

3

No one is better than Vulcan --
the smooth talking owner
of a carpet emporium
Rarely does he move from a chair
to show you the goods
in a four-storey building of
this sprawling grimy city
where he's made a fortune in
international sales
A mere turn of the
head, a snap of his fingers

and lean young boys come,
shouldering and unfurling carpets
in spacious upstairs rooms
as you feast on tea, pastries
beer, whatever you wish
Suddenly you're no longer
thinking in terms of hundreds
of dollars but thousands
Suddenly, quite mysteriously,
prices seem reasonable,
and the notion a few days ago
of spending $2500 on what you
casually might have called
a "a rug" would and might
have thought of as utter madness,
now seems a bargain
Vulcan is merely a tutor,
there to lend you a sense of well being
And in that quiet repose,
almost Zen like, he applies
no pressure at all
Hours later, you're still in control
After all, you've got the perfect "out"
But when you announce
how much you'd like to buy the carpet
but need your wife's approval --
and she's in Canada --
Vulcan doesn't blink an eye
A snap of the fingers
and something said in a language
you can't fathom
and a boy rushes in
with a telephone
and you find yourself relinquishing
the phone number of your home
and hear Vulcan greeting your wife,

"Hi, this is Vulcan calling
from Istanbul. Your husband's here
and can't decide on the color
of a carpet he's picked out."
Stunned and sheepish, I stutter
to my wife, "Hi, uh, yeah, uhm, yeah,
it's me . . . Ah, yeah . . ."
then explain my dilemma
Even so, after approval I tell Vulcan
I need dinner and time to consider
his wares, but he's one step ahead
In an instant, a young boy arrives
with steaming trays of food
Saying "No" is fruitless
I buy a $2000 carpet
then leave Vulcan to tackle
my friend who's a little
more eager than I am
After much haggling,
my friend turns and asks
which carpet he should buy
I point to one in particular
but my friend isn't interested
It's then Vulcan picks up on the moment,
 moving back to me,
"Marty, you like this carpet?"
"Yes," I admit, "but no, I'm not buying."
Vulcan is undaunted
"Give me a price, any price, and it's yours."
I tell him, "Any price?"
"Any price, Marty, any price!"
Okay, I think, I'll give him
a price, a figure so low he couldn't
possibly accept, then blurt out
"Five hundred dollars!"
With a snap of his fingers

and a few words, two young men
wrap up the carpet.
"It's yours. Take it with you!"

4

They start them early here
The day I depart Istanbul
a scruffy young boy rushes up
asking me to buy his snake
What will I do?
Play with it on the plane home?

Playing God

In a lounge at Heathrow,
killing time before flying
back to Canada
Watching a British morning
TV show comedian
urging an audience
to confide its nocturnal fantasies:
One woman dreams
of sitting on a toilet
in the midst of
a busy Manhattan street
Beside her sat another
woman with whom
she shares an engaging chat
Another stands
in an elevator
while it fills with water
Yet another remembers
diving into a pool
and emerging in a jail cell
in Mexico City,
and an older man keeps
dreaming the same
dream, keeps seeing
a woman in his dreams and
hearing an anonymous
voice shouting and
later discovers
it's a man
not a woman
In just about every
situation, we lose
control, we can't play
God, we wouldn't ever
wish to play God
We'd rather wake in the

arms of the world
doggedly declaring
it's all a dream
that life can't be
like that,
the dead are dead,
and, thank God,
we can only be ourselves